INTENTIONALLY CONSCIOUS LIVING

INTENTIONALLY CONSCIOUS LIVING

A journal with gratitude and quotes for those who CHOOSE not to sleepwalk through life

CATHY DIMARCHOS

Solutions2you Pty Ltd

Copyright © 2022 by Cathy Dimarchos

All rights reserved. No part of this book may be used or reproduced in any form whatsoever without written permission except in the case of brief quotations in critical articles or reviews.

Printed in Australia.

For more information, or to book an event, contact:
info@solutions2you.com.au
https://www.solutions2you.com.au/

Book design by Resources with Resonance
Cover design by Resources with Resonance

ISBN 978-0-6451438-0-5 (paperback)

First Edition: September 2022

DEDICATION

This journal is dedicated to you, the intentionally conscious humans who have chosen to become AWAKE and to show others the positive impact we can make on those around us. It is not always easy to be intentionally conscious because we need to pause, reflect, and consider the impact we make on ourselves and those around us.

Practising intentional consciousness involves speaking the truth, being humble, and genuinely elevating others so that they can thrive.

I am grateful to each of you that have chosen to step up and have a voice. A voice that says 'no' to what does not serve you and humanity. I am grateful to you who choose to think about future generations and how we can leave this planet in a better place, despite the challenges we may face today. I am grateful that you have seen, as I have, that we can leave behind something better than we found when we first began our journey.

I am also grateful to my parents, who showed me that living life to serve others brings joy. I can think of no better legacy than to show others this too.

Thank you.

"When we rise, it is important to also lift those around us."

Cathy Dimarchos

ABOUT THE AUTHOR

Cathy Dimarchos is known as the alchemist in business. She is a global, award-winning advisor, mentor and coach, humanitarian, TEDx speaker, and author. Future-focused, she thrives on developing ethical, conscious leaders and elevating everyone she works with to think BIGGER. Intent on creating IMPACT, Cathy is an indefatigable philanthropist and believes we can all contribute to lifting the baseline of people worldwide. Her legacy is to elevate humanity consciously.

VIII - ABOUT THE AUTHOR

Cathy's company, Solutions2you, was born from her passion for changing how we do business and creating a circular economy while serving others and leaving a lasting imprint. In this way, she establishes pathways that enable all people to lead the lives they deserve.

As a professional advisor and motivational voice with more than three decades of experience in finance and business, and 15 years as a qualified councillor, she is highly sought after by executives and people seeking high performance. Cathy dedicates her time to sharing knowledge that combines people, business, and situational skills. Here she delivers tangible tools so leaders can thrive and accelerate growth with practical and sustainable outcomes.

Her values take centre stage, and as a result, relationships and business become honest and expressive. She has clear boundaries in life and work and, with her values front and centre, steps forward into every challenge knowing the impact she can create.

Cathy's success stories come from supporting people to be comfortable with being uncomfortable, to unlearn patterns that don't serve them and to bring clarity to their goals. With empathy and strategic positioning, she empowers people to establish healthy professional boundaries, to think limitlessly and challenge norms.

ABOUT THE AUTHOR

Cathy's book Same People, Different Vision is an Amazon #1 Best Seller and has been awarded a Gold Prize Award for Business and Leadership and has been given a 5-star rating. This book is filled with tips and tools for leaders of all ages to shape a better tomorrow.

Cathy has also released two other anthologies in books titled Going Against the Grain and Think Limitlessly – showcasing authors across the globe who dared to be different, dream big and succeed.

CONTENTS

Dedication	v
ABOUT THE AUTHOR	vii
COLLABORATION FOR GLOBAL IMPACT	1
ARE YOU SLEEPWALKING THROUGH LIFE?	5
WHAT IS CONSCIOUS INTENTION?	7
HOW DO WE KNOW WHEN WE ARE SLEEPWALKING?	10
PURPOSE ALONE IS NOT ENOUGH	13
INFLUENCER OR INFLUENCING?	15
IT STARTS WITH OUR YOUTH	17
HOW TO USE THIS JOURNAL	20
YOUR THOUGHTS AND REFLECTIONS	22
THE AWAKENING	379

COLLABORATION FOR GLOBAL IMPACT

Cathy has said her initial trip to East Africa was one of her greatest challenges but has also proven to be the most rewarding. Her time living with the Maasai, building water tanks, teaching English and working in orphanages and baby crisis centres enabled her to crystalise her vision of 'paying it forward.'

With 10% of the poor living in Africa in 1970, we had the chance to create change for those living in impoverished conditions. Instead, we have continued doing what the West saw as right rather than what Africa actually needed. This demographic has increased exponentially over the last decade, to 75%, and alarmingly, it is predicted to reach 90% by 2030. A staggering statistic by anyone's reckoning. The Western world provides aid but leaves behind the opportunity to make each African country self-reliant and sustainable. We forget that along with aid, communities need support to keep their culture vibrant and alive and to be encouraged to lead through education. Leadership is most effective when it comes from within, with solid foundations based on shared knowledge that provides critical thinking at grassroots levels and across generations. Sadly, we have operated on the model of 'giving people a fish' rather than 'teaching people to fish.'

2 – CATHY DIMARCHOS

The world population is expanding far greater in Africa than on any other continent. Not helping them succeed in living life means we are impacting humanity globally. We must stop over-consumption and educate to create self-reliance. We can no longer deny that we are contributing to the cata-strophic outcomes escalating across Africa.

Starvation is real, and famine will become even more widespread. The rich will become richer, and the poor will continue to become poorer. By providing meagre aid or not doing anything at all, we are not only creating class divisions in the Western world but also creating class divisions across countries. Somehow many seem to think it's ok – because it's not on our 'turf.'

If we are to elevate humanity, we must work where it is needed the most so that we can all rise and live life from a higher baseline. We are only as strong, healthy, and smart as the weakest part of humanity, and we can no longer afford to ignore what is blatantly apparent.

No matter your life's journey, know that you always have choices. A choice to leave behind what is not serving you and choice in who you choose to be. Choice is about responding not reacting, and choice is in the ripple you create. Choose wisely where your time, energy and focus goes. Our awaken-ings can come at any time and in any place. The conscious intention we apply to understand them will be the greatest gift we give to ourselves and humanity at large. Remember that each of us, no matter how insignificant we may feel at times, has the potential to create many positive ripples in the world. Especially when we collaborate for global impact.

Cathy has made several trips to Africa since 2014, supporting young leaders and entrepreneurs on the ground through **Raise the Baseline,** *a project she developed. Through this training, individuals are given the skills they need to shape a better tomorrow – for themselves and the global community. The steps necessary to expand Cathy's vision become clearer every time she asks herself, "What else?" and, "How can I think bigger?"*

4 – CATHY DIMARCHOS

Staying intentionally conscious as she answers these questions has allowed her to broaden the impact she can make. You can find out more about Cathy's program, **Raise the Baseline***, and its ripple effect at https://www.solutions2you.com.au/raise-the-baseline.*

ARE YOU SLEEPWALKING THROUGH LIFE?

In a world where buzzwords like awakened, enlightened and woke litter conversations and media coverage, it is easy to believe we know what's happening. We can fool ourselves that we are a part of the solution, not the problem because we agree with a news reader or social media post. Heck, we may even be moved to action; to sign a petition, align with a sentiment, or share a relevant video.

But how much do we really know? How much of what we hear are we actually applying to our lives? Do we know what these ideas really mean to us, our values, and our daily choices? Or are we Sleepwalking through life?

We can live without complication, only 'knowing what we know.' We get both satisfaction and relief from planning our lives around this knowledge. We take comfort from the fact that we have 'thought ahead,' 'planned for our future,' and 'considered our options' – not even considering there might be more to the picture.

It is conscientious to have 'done the work' to get to this point, but we will continue to Sleepwalk if we don't take it a step further. The step we must take is not just becoming conscious of our beliefs, decisions, and actions; it is about becoming intentionally conscious of them. And this makes all the difference.

This journal is one of many tools you can use to determine if – or where – you are Sleepwalking Through Life. Use it as a reflective vessel to ex-lore what you uncover on your journey to becoming intentionally conscious.

Cathy often shares her vision on how being intentionally conscious is about taking that one step more, then and there, that creates that positive ripple. You can find out more and follow her for further motivation through various social media handles by looking up 'Cathy Dimarchos' or 'Solutions2you' across different platforms.

WHAT IS CONSCIOUS INTENTION?

So, what is conscious intention, and why should you want to live with it?

When we are prepared to be present, we open ourselves up to wonderful opportunities. Being comfortable with being uncomfortable breaks through barriers to awaken us.

Consider that each one of us is like one drop of water falling into a larger body of water. Every drop creates a ripple effect that is made up of our choices and our actions, whether we are aware of it or not. Regardless of whether these ripples are negative or positive, they reverberate out and bounce back. That's the impact we have on ourselves and each other.

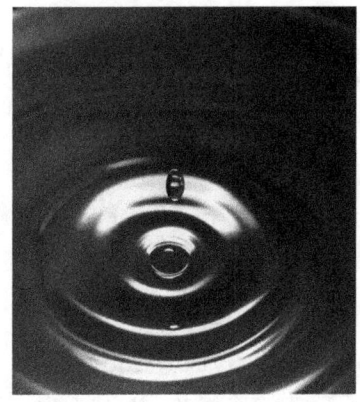

Together, as those raindrops, we can collectively raise that body of water so that anyone and anything in it rises at the same time. Being conscious with intention is about choosing to show others what you know as

8 – CATHY DIMARCHOS

you rise, not waiting until you get to a higher place (with more information, more skill or more experience) before sharing your knowledge.

It is about making a choice that benefits someone else in that moment, not about what you will gain by knowing or doing something first. Showing our future generation what is possible whilst they are still young will allow them to make better choices as they navigate life. Rather than saying, "Wait till you are a little older," or worse still, "Wait your turn," we can lead by example and include others so that we can all grow together.

Unearthing the truth, sharing failings and taking away the lessons is a celebration because we chose to do something new. Encouraging differences and learning to accept our own bias – and be ok with it – is about being intentionally conscious. Living this way allows us to live a life with equality, compassion and the ability to be beyond resilient – to be antifragile – so that we can become stronger from all our experiences.

Being prepared to present the whole of ourselves, publicly and vulnerably, is being conscious with intention. In this way, those around us know we don't always have it all, and we don't always have it all together.

It is easy to believe we are awake to life, but how often each day do you consider the global impact of your decisions? Our drives for success may be noble and well-warranted, but it's possible they are primarily self-focused. When that post comes up in your social media feed, do you instantly share it with your network? Do you hand out your 'likes' to everything you scroll past so that you feel like you belong? How often do you take the time to consider the original source of what you read, hear, or watch and ensure that it aligns with your values? Or that it doesn't breach your boundaries? We often say what we think others want to hear so we can feel accepted. Becoming aware of moments like these allows us to bring greater depth and consciousness to our experiences.

We all have lived experiences we can draw on to help us stay awake, so as you share this journey with me, know that you are choosing to be conscious with intention.

HOW DO WE KNOW WHEN WE ARE SLEEPWALKING?

When we add things to our lives, we must let other things go, it is the way we get flow. The choices we make about what we include in our lives are just as important as what we exclude. If we allow 'life' or others to make these decisions for us, we live in autopilot. Not choosing is still a choice and has consequences we may or may not be able to predict. Sadly, choosing to stay asleep often leads to unnecessary pain, be it mental or physical.

When we give ourselves the opportunity to discover what we value and want to experience, we allow ourselves the freedom to make choices that serve us and others around us. We stop sleepwalking through life. Turning autopilot off opens opportunities to live intentionally conscious and with purpose.

Answering the following questions will give you clues about places you may be sleepwalking through. If you feel triggered by a question or can definitely point to an event that rings true when you answer the question, spend a little time journalling about your thoughts and feelings.

See if you can look at each situation that arises from multiple perspectives (remember we all have our own subconscious biases). Be honest about any role you may have played (we all contribute to every situation). Can you bring some intentional consciousness to your feelings and reactions? What can you do to remind yourself of how you'd like to respond if a similar problem arises in the future? Immediate action is one way to bring intentional consciousness to a situation.

ARE YOU SLEEPWALKING?

Can you articulate your values?
Do you avoid or ignore difficult conversations because they are uncomfortable?
Have you paused to consider the wider ramifications of your decisions or actions?
Do you hope someone else will take action, so you
don't have to?
Are you pleasing someone else at the expense of
yourself?Do you ever feel out of alignment with your values or beliefs?
Do you take responsibility for correcting something
when you are wrong?
Are you ready to be seen for who you choose to be?
Is what you've heard a 'story' you have been sold?

ARE YOU READY TO CREATE A POSITIVE RIPPLE EFFECT?

Ask yourself these questions when you come to a choice point:

> Will this decision/action be life-enhancing for me and others?
> Who else might this choice affect?
> Could this action have a negative effect on others?
> Is there another choice I can make to achieve this end that has a more positive impact on others?
> Who or what is my money supporting when I make that purchase?
> Does this choice align with my values?
> Am I inadvertently supporting something that is in opposition to what I value?
> Is this decision/action taking me closer to where I want to be or farther away?

When we make decisions and take actions that are in alignment with our values and beliefs, we live a life with joy, and we radiate positive ripples into the world. The more we practise, the easier it gets. The more we apply these principles, the more significant the positive impact we can make.

"The more you praise and celebrate in life, the more there is to celebrate." Oprah Winfrey

PURPOSE ALONE IS NOT ENOUGH

There is a lot of talk in business and leadership circles about purpose. Mostly, it centres on using your purpose (as opposed to just your mission statement or values) to help drive success. Whilst this is a step closer to a holistic approach, it is far from all that is required.

Saying you know your 'why' does not automatically enlighten you. Far too many people have given the topic consideration and created powerful statements. Still, unless these are used to make choices and change limiting patterns, their effect is little more than lip service.

Knowing your purpose is critical, but unless you know what impact you want that purpose to achieve, it may be holding you back. Until you can couple your purpose with engaging and measurable actions, you will have limited your ability to create change.

It is the act of doing that begins the value proposition of your purpose. It is then the realisation of what it has done for someone else. Only then is purpose most significant. Like much of what this journal asks you to consider, applying intentional consciousness to your purpose can give you, it, and humanity the boost it needs to create lasting positive change.

"There is no greater gift you can give or receive than to honour your calling." Oprah Winfrey

INFLUENCER OR INFLUENCING?

In our digital age, much of popular culture revolves around influencers. We know about a brand, product, or idea because we have heard it mentioned in social or traditional media. But do you ever wonder why that brand, product, or idea is in your field? Was someone paid to 'influence' your thoughts? And does the answer to that question change how you now relate to that brand, product, or idea?

The speed of our modern media cycle and the functionality of the platforms we consume content on encourages us to feast on a ceaseless stream of information. For some of that data to create an impact for its creators, certain people are hand-picked to deliver their messages. Chosen for their appeal to the audience in question, these influencers do their best to promote the brand, product, or idea that pays their bills –irrespective of its intrinsic worth to the consumer.

Even if they do lead a group of devotees, being an influencer is ultimately about self-promotion. It often meets the short-term goals of those who participate but has little to do with purposeful leadership. Influencing, on the other hand, is about supporting and elevating others.

16 – CATHY DIMARCHOS

When we influence for impact, we show others, step-by-step, how to do something. This is the key to creating a more significant positive ripple than can be achieved on one's own. True leaders develop more leaders and are not afraid to become redundant. They don't seek to be influencers; they seek to influence for purpose and impact. Ego is put to the side, as this elevates others, not themselves.

Contributing to something greater than ourselves and be-coming comfortable taking others on the journey helps build trust and makes people feel like they belong. Better still, this approach lets others know they can do it too. Gratefully, the tide of influencers seems to be set to change.

Generation Alpha (those born from 2010 onward) are showing a deeper understanding of our shared humanity than many of the generations that have gone before. They are already taking action beyond self-image to create positive global impacts.

So, will you be an influencer of a person of influence? Who will be on the journey with you? And how can you bring your intentional consciousness to this equation?

IT STARTS WITH OUR YOUTH

It is essential to listen to what is not said, as much as what is said, no matter who we speak with. It is in this space that we begin to truly recognise who we are in the presence of and the impact they are capable of making. Whilst children being 'seen and not heard' has mostly dissolved from our day-to-day lives, there are arenas where this is not only prevalent, but dangerous to our shared future.

It is not a stretch to say that our nations' children are the future. They will be the decision-makers, the policy creators, and the custodians of our lives and environment as we grow older. Yet, what are they being taught? The often-fragmented version of reality some burden our children with leaves little room for growth.

We are living in a cosmic cycle where the choices we make will either create a greater division for humanity or bring us closer together. If we hope to thrive long-term as a global community, we must encourage our youth to embrace our shared humanity. To live out their personal missions with the same positive ripple effects we hope to make.

18 – CATHY DIMARCHOS

To achieve this, our youth need a voice; they need an opportunity to sit at the table and be heard. While we are in a position to do so, we must change policies to serve those working and living at grassroots levels. We must promote education that encourages critical thinking, not just book-smarts or behind-desk skills.

When we can model antifragility rather than simply resilience – and show young people how to gain strength from adversity, rather than just living through it – we will provide them with the knowledge to create great change. Risk-averse 'old heads' should be encouraged to not only share their wisdom but also to hand over the reins because change is necessary for societies to flourish.

INTENTIONALLY CONSCIOUS LIVING – 19

Our youth can go well beyond the 'what was' that we were trained to work with. They have the power and insight to work toward 'what needs to be' and 'what is ahead.' They need to be encouraged to experiment and experience failure, to take the lessons away from each curveball that comes their way. That way, we can truly innovate and create communities that recognise and value our shared humanity and the planet on which it exists.

When we value the role our youth play and are prepared to stay in pursuit of what is important, we will achieve the impossible. Coupling this mindset with our growing ability to remain intentionally conscious helps us develop limitless beliefs and provides countless opportunities for growth and compassionate service.

HOW TO USE THIS JOURNAL

Within these pages are inspirational and thought-provoking quotes, blank spaces to explore your thoughts, and questions to motivate gratitude and self-reflection. There are specific questions that encourage states of appreciation and positivity and allow you to notice patterns that might be limiting or life-enhancing. Recognising how you react or respond to similar situations over time is extraordinarily valuable in helping you remain intentionally conscious.

Spread evenly throughout the journal, you will find a page of prompts to help you start your week. These guide you in setting your intentions for the coming week and provide a touchstone to return to when you need a reminder or encounter a difficult situation.

To bookend the week, you'll find another page of questions and prompts that allow you to reflect on and track your progress each week.

INTENTIONALLY CONSCIOUS LIVING – 21

Creating a routine that prioritises a self-reflective practice, such as journalling, allows you to live with conscious intention. It builds in the positive reminders we all need to stay true to ourselves amid our busy lives and more readily enables us to celebrate our successes.

So, I encourage you to think, feel, write, decompress, and praise what you experience. Use this journal to awaken your-self to your choices, why you make them, and how you can use this information to stay more intentionally conscious.

Please note: There are many quotations and words of wisdom in this journal. Where not specifically attributed to someone else, questions, quotes and guidance are Cathy's suggestions for you to ponder.

Your thoughts & reflections

Set your intentions...

A shared journey creates impact and will survive us all.

Cathy Dimarchos

Start of the Week
gratitude & self-reflection

A mantra that will guide me this week
_____
_____
_____

What I choose to let go of
_____
_____
_____

This week I will spend more time on
_____
_____
_____

I will improve on
_____
_____
_____

Someone I can reach out to this week
_____
_____

BE THE CHANGE YOU WANT TO
SEE IN THE WORLD

Mahatma Gandhi

When we are prepared to stay in pursuit of what is important, we will achieve the impossible.

Cathy Dimarchos

End of the Week
gratitude & self-reflection

I found joy by
_____
_____
_____

The best thing that happened
_____
_____
_____

This week I am most grateful for
_____
_____
_____

My greatest learning this week
_____
_____
_____

Next week I will intentionally give more focus to
_____
_____

Sometimes we must give up something good to experience something better.

— Cathy Dimarchos

Start of the Week
gratitude & self-reflection

A mantra that will guide me this week
_____
_____
_____

What I choose to let go of
_____
_____
_____

This week I will spend more time on
_____
_____
_____

I will improve on
_____
_____
_____

Someone I can reach out to this week
_____
_____

DON'T SLEEPWALK THROUGH LIFE. BE INTENTIONALLY CONSCIOUS SO YOU KNOW THE IMPACT YOUR LIFE CAN HAVE.

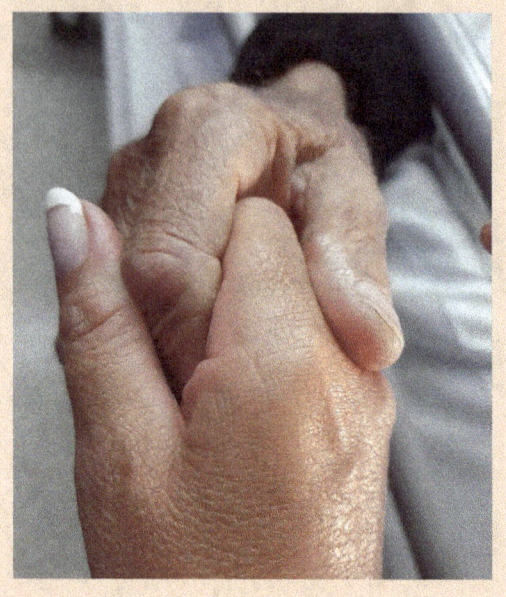

Listen to what is not said, just as much as what is said. That is where we begin to truly recognise who we are in the presence of.

Cathy Dimarchos

INTENTIONALLY CONSCIOUS LIVING

40 — CATHY DIMARCHOS

42 - CATHY DIMARCHOS

End of the Week
gratitude & self-reflection

I found joy by
_____
_____
_____

The best thing that happened
_____
_____
_____

This week I am most grateful for
_____
_____
_____

My greatest learning this week
_____
_____
_____

Next week I will intentionally give more focus to
_____
_____

Are you thinking big enough? Ask yourself, "What else?"

— Cathy Dimarchos

Start of the Week
gratitude & self-reflection

A mantra that will guide me this week

_____
_____
_____

What I choose to let go of

_____
_____
_____

This week I will spend more time on

_____
_____
_____

I will improve on

_____
_____
_____

Someone I can reach out to this week

_____
_____

BREATHE INTO THE DISCOMFORT
OF GROWTH
WHEN IT INEVITABLY ARISES.

How we make people feel will either enable them to be a part of the change or it will cripple them. Choose wisely.

Cathy Dimarchos

50 — CATHY DIMARCHOS

52 - CATHY DIMARCHOS

End of the Week
gratitude & self-reflection

I found joy by
_____
_____
_____

The best thing that happened
_____
_____
_____

This week I am most grateful for
_____
_____
_____

My greatest learning this week
_____
_____
_____

Next week I will intentionally give more focus to
_____
_____

Wake up to what is possible.

Cathy Dimarchos

Start of the Week
gratitude & self-reflection

A mantra that will guide me this week
_____
_____
_____

What I choose to let go of
_____
_____
_____

This week I will spend more time on
_____
_____
_____

I will improve on
_____
_____
_____

Someone I can reach out to this week
_____
_____

TURN YOUR FRUSTRATION INTO MOTIVATION

"Develop success from failures.
Discouragement and failure are
two of the surest stepping stones
to success."
Dale Carnegie

INTENTIONALLY CONSCIOUS LIVING

6.0 .- . CATHY DIMARCHOS

End of the Week
gratitude & self-reflection

I found joy by
_____
_____
_____

The best thing that happened
_____
_____
_____

This week I am most grateful for
_____
_____
_____

My greatest learning this week
_____
_____
_____

Next week I will intentionally give more focus to
_____
_____

Your beliefs equal your outcomes.

— Cathy Dimarchos

Start of the Week
gratitude & self-reflection

A mantra that will guide me this week
_____
_____
_____

What I choose to let go of
_____
_____
_____

This week I will spend more time on
_____
_____
_____

I will improve on
_____
_____
_____

Someone I can reach out to this week
_____
_____

WHERE CAN YOU TAKE ACTION FOR POSITIVE IMPACT?

"The pessimist sees difficulty in every opportunity. The optimist sees opportunity in every difficulty."
Winston Churchill

INTENTIONALLY CONSCIOUS LIVING

70 — CATHY DIMARCHOS

CATHY DIMARCHOS

End of the Week
gratitude & self-reflection

I found joy by
___
___
___

The best thing that happened
___
___
___

This week I am most grateful for
___
___
___

My greatest learning this week
___
___
___

Next week I will intentionally give more focus to
___
___

A little progress each day adds up to big results.

— Unknown

Start of the Week
gratitude & self-reflection

A mantra that will guide me this week
_____
_____
_____

What I choose to let go of
_____
_____
_____

This week I will spend more time on
_____
_____
_____

I will improve on
_____
_____
_____

Someone I can reach out to this week
_____
_____

MOMENTS OF CRISIS TEND TO LEAD TO THE CLEAREST OF VISIONS.

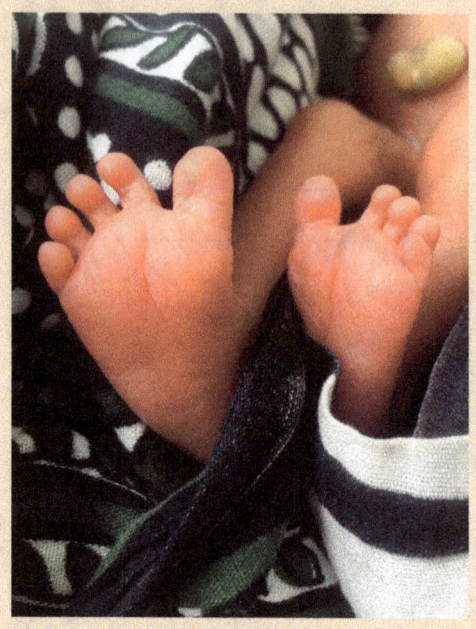

"There are three ways to ultimate success: The first way is to be kind. The second way is to be kind. The third way is to be kind."
Mister Rogers

80 - CATHY DIMARCHOS

End of the Week
gratitude & self-reflection

I found joy by
_____
_____
_____

The best thing that happened
_____
_____
_____

This week I am most grateful for
_____
_____
_____

My greatest learning this week
_____
_____
_____

Next week I will intentionally give more focus to
_____
_____

Spend time where you are celebrated.

— Kendall Williams

Start of the Week
gratitude & self-reflection

A mantra that will guide me this week
_____
_____
_____

What I choose to let go of
_____
_____
_____

This week I will spend more time on
_____
_____
_____

I will improve on
_____
_____
_____

Someone I can reach out to this week
_____
_____

INTENTIONALLY CONSCIOUS LIVING

WE FIRST NEED TO CHOOSE TO BE AWAKE AND THEN WE NEED TO ACTION WHAT WE KNOW.

Reminder: you don't need to know it all.

— Cathy Dimarchos

INTENTIONALLY CONSCIOUS LIVING

90 .-. CATHY DIMARCHOS.

CATHY DIMARCHOS

End of the Week
gratitude & self-reflection

I found joy by
_____
_____
_____

The best thing that happened
_____
_____
_____

This week I am most grateful for
_____
_____
_____

My greatest learning this week
_____
_____
_____

Next week I will intentionally give more focus to
_____
_____

Listen to the voice of nature. It holds treasures for you.

Huron

Start of the Week
gratitude & self-reflection

A mantra that will guide me this week
_____
_____
_____

What I choose to let go of
_____
_____
_____

This week I will spend more time on
_____
_____
_____

I will improve on
_____
_____
_____

Someone I can reach out to this week
_____
_____

RECOGNISE TRIGGERS,
DON'T HOLD ON TO THEM.

When we choose to embrace the journey and trust love and joy, we are free to fly.
Annicken R Day

INTENTIONALLY CONSCIOUS LIVING

100 - CATHY DIMARCHOS

End of the Week
gratitude & self-reflection

I found joy by
_____
_____
_____

The best thing that happened
_____
_____
_____

This week I am most grateful for
_____
_____
_____

My greatest learning this week
_____
_____
_____

Next week I will intentionally give more focus to
_____
_____

WHAT STORY ARE YOU BEING SOLD? IS IT TRUE?

Start of the Week
gratitude & self-reflection

A mantra that will guide me this week
_____
_____
_____

What I choose to let go of
_____
_____
_____

This week I will spend more time on
_____
_____
_____

I will improve on
_____
_____
_____

Someone I can reach out to this week
_____
_____

Pause and breathe into what was and what will be.

Cathy Dimarchos

INTENTIONALLY CONSCIOUS LIVING - 109

End of the Week
gratitude & self-reflection

I found joy by
_____
_____
_____

The best thing that happened
_____
_____
_____

This week I am most grateful for
_____
_____
_____

My greatest learning this week
_____
_____
_____

Next week I will intentionally give more focus to
_____
_____

Don't be afraid to go against the grain

Cathy Dimarchos

Start of the Week
gratitude & self-reflection

A mantra that will guide me this week
_____
_____
_____

What I choose to let go of
_____
_____
_____

This week I will spend more time on
_____
_____
_____

I will improve on
_____
_____
_____

Someone I can reach out to this week
_____
_____

INTENTIONALLY CONSCIOUS LIVING

WHAT STORY ARE YOU TELLING YOURSELF?

To live life with abundance is to live life with influence so that others may reach destinations you are yet to reach.

Cathy Dimarchos

CATHY DIMARCHOS

INTENTIONALLY CONSCIOUS LIVING - 1-19

INTENTIONALLY CONSCIOUS LIVING — 121

End of the Week
gratitude & self-reflection

I found joy by

_____
_____
_____

The best thing that happened

_____
_____
_____

This week I am most grateful for

_____
_____
_____

My greatest learning this week

_____
_____
_____

Next week I will intentionally give more focus to

_____
_____

There is always light

If only we are brave

enough to see it

If only we are brave

enough to be it.

Amanda Gorman

Start of the Week
gratitude & self-reflection

A mantra that will guide me this week
_____
_____
_____

What I choose to let go of
_____
_____
_____

This week I will spend more time on
_____
_____
_____

I will improve on
_____
_____
_____

Someone I can reach out to this week
_____
_____

INTENTIONALLY CONSCIOUS LIVING — 125

> DON'T COMPARE YOUR INTERNAL REALITY TO SOMEONE ELSE'S EXTERNAL REPRESENTATION

Being comfortable with being uncomfortable breaks through barriers to awaken us.

Cathy Dimarchos

128 - CATHY DIMARCHOS

End of the Week
gratitude & self-reflection

I found joy by
_____
_____
_____

The best thing that happened
_____
_____
_____

This week I am most grateful for
_____
_____
_____

My greatest learning this week
_____
_____
_____

Next week I will intentionally give more focus to
_____
_____

The path forward does not have to be straight – it just needs to be the one that's right for you.

— Cathy Dimarchos

Start of the Week
gratitude & self-reflection

A mantra that will guide me this week

_____
_____
_____

What I choose to let go of

_____
_____
_____

This week I will spend more time on

_____
_____
_____

I will improve on

_____
_____
_____

Someone I can reach out to this week

_____
_____

WHAT IS YOUR INNER GUIDANCE TRYING TO TELL YOU?

Your beliefs

equal

your outcomes

Cathy Dimarchos

138 - CATHY DIMARCHOS

End of the Week
gratitude & self-reflection

I found joy by
_____
_____
_____

The best thing that happened
_____
_____
_____

This week I am most grateful for
_____
_____
_____

My greatest learning this week
_____
_____
_____

Next week I will intentionally give more focus to
_____
_____

Pay it forward.

— Lily Hardy Hammond

Start of the Week
gratitude & self-reflection

A mantra that will guide me this week
___
___
___

What I choose to let go of
___
___
___

This week I will spend more time on
___
___
___

I will improve on
___
___
___

Someone I can reach out to this week
___
___

DO YOU HAVE BOUNDARIES AROUND WHERE YOU PLACE YOUR TIME, ENERGY, AND FOCUS?

Being conscious and having purpose alone are not enough. Being intentionally conscious and being purposeful to create impact for others is where you begin.

Cathy Dimarchos

148 .- CATHY DIMARCHOS

End of the Week
gratitude & self-reflection

I found joy by
_____
_____
_____

The best thing that happened
_____
_____
_____

This week I am most grateful for
_____
_____
_____

My greatest learning this week
_____
_____
_____

Next week I will intentionally give more focus to
_____
_____

Choose to step forward knowing the impact you can create by elevating others.

Cathy Dimarchos

Start of the Week
gratitude & self-reflection

A mantra that will guide me this week
_____
_____
_____

What I choose to let go of
_____
_____
_____

This week I will spend more time on
_____
_____
_____

I will improve on
_____
_____
_____

Someone I can reach out to this week
_____
_____

ACKNOWLEDGE YOUR TRUTH,
THEN APPLY WHAT YOU KNOW.

Those that succeed ask for help and have skin in the game.

Cathy Dimarchos

CATHY DIMARCHOS

End of the Week
gratitude & self-reflection

I found joy by
_____
_____
_____

The best thing that happened
_____
_____
_____

This week I am most grateful for
_____
_____
_____

My greatest learning this week
_____
_____
_____

Next week I will intentionally give more focus to
_____
_____

We all have many sides, and we can embody them all.

Cathy Dimarchos

Start of the Week
gratitude & self-reflection

A mantra that will guide me this week
_____
_____
_____

What I choose to let go of
_____
_____
_____

This week I will spend more time on
_____
_____
_____

I will improve on
_____
_____
_____

Someone I can reach out to this week
_____
_____

ARE YOUR BOUNDARIES SERVING YOU?

If you remember why you started, then you will know why you must continue.
Chris Burkmenn

INTENTIONALLY CONSCIOUS LIVING

168 – CATHY DIMARCHOS

170 - CATHY DIMARCHOS

End of the Week
gratitude & self-reflection

I found joy by
_____
_____
_____

The best thing that happened
_____
_____
_____

This week I am most grateful for
_____
_____
_____

My greatest learning this week
_____
_____
_____

Next week I will intentionally give more focus to
_____
_____

It always seems impossible until it's done.

— *Nelson Mandela*

Start of the Week
gratitude & self-reflection

A mantra that will guide me this week
_____
_____
_____

What I choose to let go of
_____
_____
_____

This week I will spend more time on
_____
_____
_____

I will improve on
_____
_____
_____

Someone I can reach out to this week
_____
_____

INSPIRATION
WITHOUT ACTION
IS WASTED POTENTIAL.

CATHY DIMARCHOS

You have the power to protect your peace.
Unknown

INTENTIONALLY CONSCIOUS LIVING

1.78. -. CATHY DI.MARCHOS

End of the Week
gratitude & self-reflection

I found joy by
_____
_____
_____

The best thing that happened
_____
_____
_____

This week I am most grateful for
_____
_____
_____

My greatest learning this week
_____
_____
_____

Next week I will intentionally give more focus to
_____
_____

When we add things into our lives, we must let other things go.

Cathy Dimarchos

Start of the Week
gratitude & self-reflection

A mantra that will guide me this week
___
___
___

What I choose to let go of
___
___
___

This week I will spend more time on
___
___
___

I will improve on
___
___
___

Someone I can reach out to this week
___
___

ACKNOWLEDGE WHAT'S OUT OF BALANCE IN YOUR LIFE AND COMMIT TO ADJUSTING IT.

Nothing ever goes away until it teaches us what we need to know.

Pema Chodron

INTENTIONALLY CONSCIOUS LIVING

188 - CATHY DIMARCHOS

End of the Week
gratitude & self-reflection

I found joy by
_____
_____
_____

The best thing that happened
_____
_____
_____

This week I am most grateful for
_____
_____
_____

My greatest learning this week
_____
_____
_____

Next week I will intentionally give more focus to
_____
_____

Will you think limitlessly?

— Cathy Dimarchos

Start of the Week
gratitude & self-reflection

A mantra that will guide me this week
_____
_____
_____

What I choose to let go of
_____
_____
_____

This week I will spend more time on
_____
_____
_____

I will improve on
_____
_____
_____

Someone I can reach out to this week
_____
_____

CAN YOU REINVIGORATE
A DREAM
YOU HAVE LET GO OF?

More is lost by indecision than wrong decision.
Marcus Tullius Cicero

INTENTIONALLY CONSCIOUS LIVING

198 .- . CATHY DIMARCHOS

End of the Week
gratitude & self-reflection

I found joy by
_____
_____
_____

The best thing that happened
_____
_____
_____

This week I am most grateful for
_____
_____
_____

My greatest learning this week
_____
_____
_____

Next week I will intentionally give more focus to
_____
_____

Just about everyone can get to 95% - however not everyone is willing to do what it takes to get to 100%

Cathy Dimarchos

Start of the Week
gratitude & self-reflection

A mantra that will guide me this week
_____
_____
_____

What I choose to let go of
_____
_____
_____

This week I will spend more time on
_____
_____
_____

I will improve on
_____
_____
_____

Someone I can reach out to this week
_____
_____

WHERE CAN YOU BRING MORE BALANCE TO YOUR LIFESTYLE?

*Start where you are.
Use what you have.
Do what you can.*
— Arthur Ashe

INTENTIONALLY CONSCIOUS LIVING - 207

208. -. CATHY DIMARCHOS

End of the Week
gratitude & self-reflection

I found joy by
_____
_____
_____

The best thing that happened
_____
_____
_____

This week I am most grateful for
_____
_____
_____

My greatest learning this week
_____
_____
_____

Next week I will intentionally give more focus to
_____
_____

Be more than Resilient – become antifragile so that you strengthen from what you have experienced.

Cathy Dimarchos

Start of the Week
gratitude & self-reflection

A mantra that will guide me this week
_____
_____
_____

What I choose to let go of
_____
_____
_____

This week I will spend more time on
_____
_____
_____

I will improve on
_____
_____
_____

Someone I can reach out to this week
_____
_____

ARE THERE PAST LESSONS YOU CAN NOW BEGIN TO ASSIMILATE?

Never give up on a dream just because of the time it will take to accomplish it. The time will pass anyway.
Earl Nightingale

… INTENTIONALLY CONSCIOUS LIVING — 217

218 ~ CATHY DIMARCHOS

220 — CATHY DIMARCHOS

End of the Week
gratitude & self-reflection

I found joy by
_____
_____
_____

The best thing that happened
_____
_____
_____

This week I am most grateful for
_____
_____
_____

My greatest learning this week
_____
_____
_____

Next week I will intentionally give more focus to
_____
_____

When we live with Conscious Intention we can respond rather than react to our circumstances.

Cathy Dimarchos

Start of the Week
gratitude & self-reflection

A mantra that will guide me this week
_____
_____
_____

What I choose to let go of
_____
_____
_____

This week I will spend more time on
_____
_____
_____

I will improve on
_____
_____
_____

Someone I can reach out to this week
_____
_____

TRUE LEADERS DEVELOP MORE LEADERS AND ARE NOT AFRAID TO BECOME REDUNDANT, BECAUSE THERE ARE ALWAYS MORE PEOPLE TO DEVELOP.

Our greatest glory is not in never falling, but in rising every time we fall.
Confucius

INTENTIONALLY CONSCIOUS LIVING

228 — CATHY DIMARCHOS

End of the Week
gratitude & self-reflection

I found joy by
_____
_____
_____

The best thing that happened
_____
_____
_____

This week I am most grateful for
_____
_____
_____

My greatest learning this week
_____
_____
_____

Next week I will intentionally give more focus to
_____
_____

Influencing for impact is about supporting and elevating others. Being an influencer is about self-promotion.

Cathy Dimarchos

Start of the Week
gratitude & self-reflection

A mantra that will guide me this week
_____
_____
_____

What I choose to let go of
_____
_____
_____

This week I will spend more time on
_____
_____
_____

I will improve on
_____
_____
_____

Someone I can reach out to this week
_____
_____

> WE NEED TO MAKE CHOICES ABOUT WHAT WE WANT IN LIFE, JUST AS MUCH AS WHAT WE DON'T WANT IN LIFE.

Courage is the most important of all the virtues because without courage, you can't practice any other virtue consistently.
Maya Angelou

INTENTIONALLY CONSCIOUS LIVING

238 — CATHY DIMARCHOS

End of the Week
gratitude & self-reflection

I found joy by
_____
_____
_____

The best thing that happened
_____
_____
_____

This week I am most grateful for
_____
_____
_____

My greatest learning this week
_____
_____
_____

Next week I will intentionally give more focus to
_____
_____

Create a ripple that bounces back with positive universal feedback.

Cathy Dimarchos

Start of the Week
gratitude & self-reflection

A mantra that will guide me this week

_____
_____
_____

What I choose to let go of

_____
_____
_____

This week I will spend more time on

_____
_____
_____

I will improve on

_____
_____
_____

Someone I can reach out to this week

_____
_____

INTENTIONALLY CONSCIOUS LIVING

> **WHEN WE LIVE OUR LIFE IN AUTOPILOT, WE "SLEEPWALK THROUGH LIFE."**

We must reach out our hand in friendship and dignity both to those who would befriend us and those who would be our enemy.

Arthur Ashe

INTENTIONALLY CONSCIOUS LIVING

248 — CATHY DIMARCHOS

End of the Week
gratitude & self-reflection

I found joy by
_____
_____
_____

The best thing that happened
_____
_____
_____

This week I am most grateful for
_____
_____
_____

My greatest learning this week
_____
_____
_____

Next week I will intentionally give more focus to
_____
_____

Act as if what you do makes a difference, because it does.
— William James

Start of the Week
gratitude & self-reflection

A mantra that will guide me this week
_____
_____
_____

What I choose to let go of
_____
_____
_____

This week I will spend more time on
_____
_____
_____

I will improve on
_____
_____
_____

Someone I can reach out to this week
_____
_____

"IT IS NOT THE MOUNTAIN WE
CONQUER, BUT OURSELVES".
EDMUND HILLARY

Remember, teamwork begins by building trust. And the only way to do that is to overcome our need for invulnerability.
Patrick Lencioni

INTENTIONALLY CONSCIOUS LIVING

258 – CATHY DIMARCHOS

End of the Week
gratitude & self-reflection

I found joy by
_____
_____
_____

The best thing that happened
_____
_____
_____

This week I am most grateful for
_____
_____
_____

My greatest learning this week
_____
_____
_____

Next week I will intentionally give more focus to
_____
_____

Collaborate

for

global impact.

Cathy Dimarchos

Start of the Week
gratitude & self-reflection

A mantra that will guide me this week

_____
_____
_____

What I choose to let go of

_____
_____
_____

This week I will spend more time on

_____
_____
_____

I will improve on

_____
_____
_____

Someone I can reach out to this week

_____
_____

SHOWING OTHERS HOW TO DO SOMETHING, STEP-BY-STEP, IS THE KEY TO CREATING A GREATER RIPPLE EFFECT.

Somewhere, something incredible is waiting to be known.
Carl Sagan

INTENTIONALLY CONSCIOUS LIVING

268. – CATHY DIMARCHOS

End of the Week
gratitude & self-reflection

I found joy by
_____
_____
_____

The best thing that happened
_____
_____
_____

This week I am most grateful for
_____
_____
_____

My greatest learning this week
_____
_____
_____

Next week I will intentionally give more focus to
_____
_____

Gratitude turns what we have into enough. It turns denial into acceptance, chaos into order, confusion into clarity. It makes sense of our past, brings peace for today, and creates a vision for tomorrow.

Melody Beattie

Start of the Week
gratitude & self-reflection

A mantra that will guide me this week

_____
_____
_____

What I choose to let go of

_____
_____
_____

This week I will spend more time on

_____
_____
_____

I will improve on

_____
_____
_____

Someone I can reach out to this week

_____
_____

LIVE A LIFE THAT HONOURS EQUALITY, COMPASSION AND THE ABILITY TO BE BEYOND RESILIENT. BE "ANTIFRAGILE" & LEARN FROM WHAT HAS FAILED, THEN STRENGTHEN FROM IT.

The greatest discovery of my generation is that a human being can alter his life by altering his attitudes.
William James

278 – CATHY DIMARCHOS

End of the Week
gratitude & self-reflection

I found joy by
_____
_____
_____

The best thing that happened
_____
_____
_____

This week I am most grateful for
_____
_____
_____

My greatest learning this week
_____
_____
_____

Next week I will intentionally give more focus to
_____
_____

What are you aware of that you are not actioning?

Is this serving you?

Cathy Dimarchos

Start of the Week
gratitude & self-reflection

A mantra that will guide me this week
_____
_____
_____

What I choose to let go of
_____
_____
_____

This week I will spend more time on
_____
_____
_____

I will improve on
_____
_____
_____

Someone I can reach out to this week
_____
_____

INFLUENCE FOR IMPACT

It is never too late to be what you might have been.

George Eliot

288 - CATHY DIMARCHOS

End of the Week
gratitude & self-reflection

I found joy by
_____
_____
_____

The best thing that happened
_____
_____
_____

This week I am most grateful for
_____
_____
_____

My greatest learning this week
_____
_____
_____

Next week I will intentionally give more focus to
_____
_____

Being comfortable to take others on the journey with you, openly and freely, whilst scary at times for being made redundant, is the only way to build trust and to make people feel like they belong.

Cathy Dimarchos

Start of the Week
gratitude & self-reflection

A mantra that will guide me this week
_____
_____
_____

What I choose to let go of
_____
_____
_____

This week I will spend more time on
_____
_____
_____

I will improve on
_____
_____
_____

Someone I can reach out to this week
_____
_____

> AS PEOPLE AROUND YOU LEARN THE ART OF SPEAKING, CONTINUE TO DEVELOP THE ART OF LISTENING

Stay away from those people who try to disparage your ambitions. Small minds will always do that, but great minds will give you a feeling that you can become great too.
Mark Twain

INTENTIONALLY CONSCIOUS LIVING - 297

End of the Week
gratitude & self-reflection

I found joy by
_____
_____
_____

The best thing that happened
_____
_____
_____

This week I am most grateful for
_____
_____
_____

My greatest learning this week
_____
_____
_____

Next week I will intentionally give more focus to
_____
_____

Where do you choose to be five years from now? How will you live out your life?

Cathy Dimarchos

Start of the Week
gratitude & self-reflection

A mantra that will guide me this week
_____
_____
_____

What I choose to let go of
_____
_____
_____

This week I will spend more time on
_____
_____
_____

I will improve on
_____
_____
_____

Someone I can reach out to this week
_____
_____

INTENTIONALLY CONSCIOUS LIVING - 303

DEVELOP A LIMITLESS BELIEF.

It is better to fail in originality than to succeed in imitation.
Herman Melville

306 - CATHY DIMARCHOS

INTENTIONALLY CONSCIOUS LIVING - 307

308 — CATHY DIMARCHOS

INTENTIONALLY CONSCIOUS LIVING

End of the Week
gratitude & self-reflection

I found joy by
_____
_____
_____

The best thing that happened
_____
_____
_____

This week I am most grateful for
_____
_____
_____

My greatest learning this week
_____
_____
_____

Next week I will intentionally give more focus to
_____
_____

We must find time to stop and thank the people who make a difference in our lives.

John F Kennedy

Start of the Week
gratitude & self-reflection

A mantra that will guide me this week
_____
_____
_____

What I choose to let go of
_____
_____
_____

This week I will spend more time on
_____
_____
_____

I will improve on
_____
_____
_____

Someone I can reach out to this week
_____
_____

WHERE DO YOU CHOOSE TO BE? WHO WILL BE ON THE JOURNEY WITH YOU, AND WILL YOU BE AN INFLUENCER OR A PERSON OF INFLUENCE?

Don't let someone else's opinion of you become your reality.
Les Brown

INTENTIONALLY CONSCIOUS LIVING — 317

318 - CATHY DIMARCHOS

End of the Week
gratitude & self-reflection

I found joy by
___
___
___

The best thing that happened
___
___
___

This week I am most grateful for
___
___
___

My greatest learning this week
___
___
___

Next week I will intentionally give more focus to
___
___

Live a life full of humility, gratitude, intellectual curiosity, and never stop learning.
— GZA

Start of the Week
gratitude & self-reflection

A mantra that will guide me this week
_____
_____
_____

What I choose to let go of
_____
_____
_____

This week I will spend more time on
_____
_____
_____

I will improve on
_____
_____
_____

Someone I can reach out to this week
_____
_____

> LIFE IS ABOUT NOT LEAVING THINGS BEHIND BUT PAYING THEM FORWARD, SO THAT OUR FUTURE GENERATION ENJOY A LIFE THEY DESERVE.

Inspiration does exist, but it must find you working.
Pablo Picasso

INTENTIONALLY CONSCIOUS LIVING — 327

INTENTIONALLY CONSCIOUS LIVING

End of the Week gratitude & self-reflection

I found joy by

_____
_____
_____

The best thing that happened

_____
_____
_____

This week I am most grateful for

_____
_____
_____

My greatest learning this week

_____
_____
_____

Next week I will intentionally give more focus to

_____
_____

Learn as if you will live forever, live like you will die tomorrow.

— Mahatma Gandhi

Start of the Week
gratitude & self-reflection

A mantra that will guide me this week
_____
_____
_____

What I choose to let go of
_____
_____
_____

This week I will spend more time on
_____
_____
_____

I will improve on
_____
_____
_____

Someone I can reach out to this week
_____
_____

INTENTIONALLY CONSCIOUS LIVING - 333

We are what we repeatedly do. Excellence, then, is not an act, but a habit.

Aristotle

INTENTIONALLY CONSCIOUS LIVING

336. – CATHY DIMARCHOS

End of the Week
gratitude & self-reflection

I found joy by

_____
_____
_____

The best thing that happened

_____
_____
_____

This week I am most grateful for

_____
_____
_____

My greatest learning this week

_____
_____
_____

Next week I will intentionally give more focus to

_____
_____

Your capacity to say 'No' determines your capacity to say 'Yes' to greater things.

E. Stanley Jones

Start of the Week
gratitude & self-reflection

A mantra that will guide me this week
_____
_____
_____

What I choose to let go of
_____
_____
_____

This week I will spend more time on
_____
_____
_____

I will improve on
_____
_____
_____

Someone I can reach out to this week
_____
_____

342 - CATHY DIMARCHOS

IT'S THE LESSONS WE TAKE AWAY FROM LIFE'S CURVEBALLS THAT ALLOW US TO LEARN, DEVELOP AND DO SOMETHING DIFFERENT THE NEXT TIME AROUND.

Knowing your purpose is great but unless you know what impact you want that purpose to achieve so that it is measurable and it becomes actionable, you will have limited your ability to create change.

Cathy Dimarchos

INTENTIONALLY CONSCIOUS LIVING

346 — CATHY DIMARCHOS

End of the Week
gratitude & self-reflection

I found joy by

_____
_____
_____

The best thing that happened

_____
_____
_____

This week I am most grateful for

_____
_____
_____

My greatest learning this week

_____
_____
_____

Next week I will intentionally give more focus to

_____
_____

Don't let yesterday take up too much of today.

— Will Rogers

Start of the Week
gratitude & self-reflection

A mantra that will guide me this week
_____
_____
_____

What I choose to let go of
_____
_____
_____

This week I will spend more time on
_____
_____
_____

I will improve on
_____
_____
_____

Someone I can reach out to this week
_____
_____

DON'T BE LIKE THE PERSON WHO TOLD YOU TO PLAY SMALL OR THAT YOU COULD NOT DO SOMETHING. BE THE PERSON WHO ENCOURAGES AND THEN TAKES THAT ONE STEP FURTHER - TO HELP OTHERS ACHIEVE WHAT MAY HAVE SEEMED IMPOSSIBLE.

Choose to be intentionally conscious so that as you live your life, you make choices that will create a greater impact for those around you.

Cathy Dimarchos

INTENTIONALLY CONSCIOUS LIVING

356 – CATHY DIMARCHOS

End of the Week
gratitude & self-reflection

I found joy by
_____
_____
_____

The best thing that happened
_____
_____
_____

This week I am most grateful for
_____
_____
_____

My greatest learning this week
_____
_____
_____

Next week I will intentionally give more focus to
_____
_____

If you are brave enough to say goodbye, life will reward you with a new hello.

— Paulo Coelho

Start of the Week
gratitude & self-reflection

A mantra that will guide me this week
_____
_____
_____

What I choose to let go of
_____
_____
_____

This week I will spend more time on
_____
_____
_____

I will improve on
_____
_____
_____

Someone I can reach out to this week
_____
_____

INTENTIONALLY CONSCIOUS LIVING

GO OVER OLD GROUND FOR THE SAKE OF PERSPECTIVE, NOT TO REINVIGORATE TRAUMA.

INTENTIONALLY CONSCIOUS LIVING - 363

If you want to lift yourself up, lift up someone else.

Booker T Washington

INTENTIONALLY CONSCIOUS LIVING - 365

End of the Week
gratitude & self-reflection

I found joy by
_____
_____
_____

The best thing that happened
_____
_____
_____

This week I am most grateful for
_____
_____
_____

My greatest learning this week
_____
_____
_____

Next week I will intentionally give more focus to
_____
_____

To know how much there is to know is the beginning of learning to live.

— Dorothy West

Start of the Week
gratitude & self-reflection

A mantra that will guide me this week
_____
_____
_____

What I choose to let go of
_____
_____
_____

This week I will spend more time on
_____
_____
_____

I will improve on
_____
_____
_____

Someone I can reach out to this week
_____
_____

370 - CATHY DIMARCHOS

WHEN WE CONTRIBUTE TO SOMETHING GREATER THAN OURSELVES, WE HAVE A SENSE OF PURPOSE, WE FEEL LIKE WE BELONG, AND MOST IMPORTANTLY, WE SHOW OTHERS HOW THEY CAN DO IT TOO

Teamwork is the ability to work together toward a common vision. It is the fuel that allows common people to attain uncommon results.
Andrew Carnegie

INTENTIONALLY CONSCIOUS LIVING

374 = 'CATHY DIMARCHO'S

End of the Week
gratitude & self-reflection

I found joy by
_____
_____
_____

The best thing that happened
_____
_____
_____

This week I am most grateful for
_____
_____
_____

My greatest learning this week
_____
_____
_____

Next week I will intentionally give more focus to
_____
_____

Don't ask yourself "What if?" Ask yourself "What else?" Changing that one word changes your trajectory and outlook. It changes your psyche from "doubt" to "optimism." It allows you to think about what else is possible and places you on the road to Thinking Limitlessly.

THE AWAKENING

We all awaken at different times and in different ways. I really didn't realise my conscious and intentional journey until many months after I came back from my first trip to Tanzania. You see, that trip was really about my daughter. At 16, she knew she wanted to make an impact on the world. Deciding that volunteering was the most appropriate option, she planned to travel to Tanzania, Africa, once she had turned 17 and finished school.

Now, I needed to mitigate the risks of such a trip, but I also wanted to honour her and allow her to live out her vision. I was so proud of her, but I really didn't quite understand the magnitude of this journey; not until I placed my hand on the plate glass window at the airport while she sat airside, mirroring my gesture. It was at that moment that it really dawned on me, what I had done. I had no idea where she was going. I had no idea about the terrain, the people. Nothing. And she was going to be gone for three months. Thank goodness I was going to be there with her in one month's time!

During that period there were many tears. The hardships we witnessed were previously unfathomable, and I shed tears knowing that there was so much more to be done. The real test though was to be true in each moment and actually find joy and honour the children and the families we were blessed to be living with while we were there.

I think my first real point of crystallisation was recognising my subconscious bias when I sat in the middle of Endulin, Ngorongoro, in Tanzania with the Massai. A warrior asked me, "What do you think, Cathy, this is what I'd like to do," and he began to tell me about how he wanted to shape the future for the young girls (of 11 and 12) in his community, to encourage them to hope and wish for more. I sat there and realised that I could not possibly begin to understand what he was asking of me. Nor could I begin to understand what those young girls were experiencing. Or their mothers, or grand-mothers, all living together in the same tribe. That's when it dawned on me to say, "I cannot, Kimani, really honestly answer that. I am a white Western woman with privilege." And that's when my real journey began.

Again, the magnitude of that moment really didn't play out until several months later. But with each encounter, each experience, there was an incredible knowing that there was so much more I needed to do, so much more that I needed to understand about myself, about the world. There was so much more to know about the *real* world, not about what I understood it to be.

Four months later, having come home, I was sitting with my family around the dining room table. I had been feeling troubled and I shared with them, "I hate my life!" Now, hate is such a strong word, I don't use it, but that is how I felt. The more I reflected and looked inward, the more I realised I lived such an egoic life. And there was so much more that I could contribute to the lives of others.

Now, my family sat there and looked at me, aghast with what I was saying. My son kindly shared, "Mum, you can't begrudge us for being born in the world where we have been born, because that's what you're asking us to do. But we certainly can acknowledge and use what we have and what we know to make things better somewhere else." And that's where my journey really took off.

I didn't get it right from the beginning, and I am still continuing to evolve and to better understand who I choose to be today. I pause, almost daily, to better understand who I choose to be and to reflect on the choices that I've made. I look forward and actually know where I want to be, even at my resting place. You see, I don't just look at tomorrow, at next month, or next year; I genuinely want to look at where my life will come to a close and what I want to achieve by then.

I find it absolutely amazing that our future generation, the alpha generation, the 10- and 11-year-olds, have the innate ability to look beyond what has happened over the last two or three decades - two generations - and they seem to have no trouble thinking about the collectiveness. It makes me realise that there is so much that I could have done, so now I **intentionally and consciously** think about every choice I have made and what I can do differently to ensure that as I step forward, it is in fact better. Not just for me, but for our future generation, passing lessons on to those around me, every single one of them. I'm so passionate about that, and it guides me every day.

There is nothing greater than going on that journey with someone else. At the same time, we must be respectful and mindful that each person needs to want to be there with us. Not everybody is ready to take the same journey, and that's ok. We just need to be conscious of who it is that's reaching out and asking, "Will you take me too?"

You know, as women, I'm not sure that we have quite understood that we really do need to support each other. And it's not with the intentions that I think most of us believe. It is so much deeper than that. If we are not elevating people so that they are reaching well beyond where we are today, now, before we get there ourselves, we are really not serving. See, most of us wait until we get there and then think about how to show someone else how to get there. But for me, whilst I'm learning, I'm sharing.

And I am grateful to have shared this part of my journey with you. I hope that you have also grown and evolved as you've explored your life, loves and limitations within the pages of this journal. As you continue to grow, don't forget to keep asking, "What else?"

www.ingramcontent.com/pod-product-compliance
Lightning Source LLC
Chambersburg PA
CBHW051416290426
44109CB00016B/1321